# CONTENTS

# FUNNY MUSIC JOKES

**Q:** How do you get a wedding singer off your front porch?

**A:** Pay for the pizza.


**Q:** What do you call a group of lousy singers?

**A:** A-crapella.


**Q:** What do you call an arrogant trombone player?

**A:** A brass-hole.


**Q:** What will you never say about a banjo player?

**A:** That is the banjo player's Porsche.

**Q:** How do you get a clarinet player to play louder?

A: You can't!


**Q:** What do you call a fish that needs vocal help?

A: Autotuna.


**Q:** What kind of berry plays an English horn?

A: A tooty fruity.


**Q:** How many bass players does it take to change a light bulb?

A: None. The piano player can do that with his left hand though.

**Q:** What do you call a cow that plays guitar?

**A:** A moo-sician.


**Q:** How do know a clarinet player is playing loud?

**A:** You can almost hear them.


**Q:** What music do balloons dislike?

**A:** Pop music.


**Q:** Why did the bass player get mad at the timpanist?

**A:** He turned a peg and wouldn't tell the bass player which one.

**Q:** How late does the band play?

**A:** About half a beat behind the drummer.

**Q:** Why do hummingbirds hum?

**A:** They don't know the words.

**Q:** How is a heart like a musician?

**A:** They both have a beat.

**Q:** What do you say to a punk rocker in a three piece suit?

**A:** Will the defendant please rise?

**Q:** What's the difference between a violist and a dressmaker?

**A:** A dressmaker tucks up frills.

**Q:** How do you make a bandstand?

A: Take away their chairs.


**Q:** How do you know if there is a drummer at your door?

A: The knocking always speeds up.


**Q:** Why did the boy bring a ladder to chorus?

A: He wanted to sing higher.


**Q:** Why is it difficult to get inside a piano?

A: The keys are on the inside.


**Q:** What's the definition of a nerd?

A: Someone who has his or her own alto clarinet.

**Q:** What was the name of the green singer?

A: Elvis Parsley.

**Q:** Why did they arrest the musician?

A: He got into big treble.

**Q:** What is musical and handy in the supermarket?

A: A Chopin Lizst.

**Q:** What do you get if you cross a lamp with a violin?

A: Light music.

**Q:** What do you call a mammoth who conducts an orchestra?

A: Tuskanini.

**Q:** Why did the boy who wrecked his bike in a barbed-wire fence miss his music lessons?

**A:** He had already completed the sharps and flats.

**Q:** What happened when the piano fell into the mine?

**A:** A flat minor!

**Q:** Why did the music student have a piano in the bathroom?

**A:** He was practicing Handel's Water Music.

**Q:** Why do drummers always have trouble entering a room?

**A:** They never know when to come in.

**Q:** How are pirates such great singers?

**A:** They know how to hit the high C's.

**Q:** When is the water in the shower room musical?

**A:** When it's piping hot.

**Q:** What is the difference between a cello and a coffin?

**A:** The coffin has the corpse on the inside.

**Q:** Why did the guys let the sweet potato join the band?

**A:** So they could have a yam session.

**Q:** Did you hear about the bass player who locked his keys in his car?

**A:** It took him four hours to get the drummer out.

**Q:** What is the difference between a banjo and an anchor?

**A:** You tie a rope to an anchor before you throw it overboard.

**Q:** How is playing a bagpipe like throwing a javelin blindfolded?

**A:** You don't have to be very good to get people's attention.

**Q:** What did the bagpiper score on his IQ test?

**A:** Drool.

**Q:** Why do bagpipers leave their case on the dashboards?

**A:** So they can park in handicapped zones.


**Q:** Why do bagpipers walk when they play?

**A:** To get away from the noise.


**Q:** Why did the chicken cross the road?

**A:** To get away from the bagpipe recital.


**Q:** What's an accordion good for?

**A:** Learning how to fold a map.

**Q:** How do you protect a valuable instrument?

**A:** Hide it in an accordion case.


**Q:** How do you fix a broken tuba?

**A:** With tuba glue.


**Q:** What do lead trumpet players use for birth control?

**A:** Their personality.


**Q:** What is the definition of an optimist?

**A:** An accordion player with a pager.


**Q:** What's the difference between a chainsaw and an accordion?

**A:** A chainsaw can be tuned.

**Q:** How many bass players does it take to change a light bulb?

**A:** Only one, but the guitarist has to show him first.

**Q:** How can you tell the difference between all the banjo songs?

**A:** By their names.

**Q:** What is the difference between a banjo and a chain saw?

**A:** A chain saw has a dynamic range.

**Q:** What is the difference between a Wagnerian soprano and a Wagnerian Tenor?

**A:** About 10 pounds.

**Q:** What is the missing link between the bass and the ape?

A: The baritone.


**Q:** How do you tell when your lead singer is at the door?

A: He can't find the key and doesn't know when to come in.


**Q:** Why are conductors' hearts popular for transplants?

A: They've had little use.


**Q:** Why do the singers rock left and right while performing on stage?

A: It is more difficult to hit a moving target.

**Q:** What's the definition of a quartertone?

A: A bagpiper tuning his drones.


**Q:** Why did the Boy Scout take up the banjo?

A: They make good paddles.


**Q:** What's the definition of perfect pitch?

A: When an accordion is thrown down the toilet without it touching the sides.


**Q:** Why don't they know where Mozart is buried?

A: Because he's Haydn!

**Q:** What is every cat's favorite song?

A: Three Blind Mice.

**Q:** What's the difference between an onion and an accordion?

A: No one cries when you chop up an accordion.

**Q:** What do you call a male quartet?

A: Three men and a tenor.

**Q:** What happens if you sing country music backwards?

A: You get your job and your wife back.

**Q:** What kind of music do the planets and stars listen to?

A: Nep-tunes.

**Q:** Which positions does a violist use?

**A:** First, third, and emergency.


**Q:** What is the difference between a dog and a viola?

**A:** The dog knows when to stop scratching.


**Q:** Why are orchestra intermissions only twenty minutes long?

**A:** So the violists don't need to be retrained.


**Q:** What is the most musical part of a fish?

**A:** Its scales.

**Q:** How is lightning like a violists fingers?

**A:** Neither one strikes in the same place twice.

**Q:** What is the difference between the first and last desk of a viola section?

**A:** Half a measure.

**Q:** What is the difference between a viola and a trampoline?

**A:** You take off your shoes before you jump on the trampoline.

**Q:** What do you call the musical part of a turkey?

**A:** Drumsticks.

**Q:** What is the definition of a major seventh?

A: A violist playing octaves.

**Q:** What's the difference between trumpet players and government bonds?

A: Government bonds eventually mature and earn money.

**Q:** What do you get if Bach dies and is reincarnated as twins?

A: A pair of Re-Bachs.

**Q:** What did the elves sing when Santa came back from delivering presents?

A: Freeze a jolly good fellow!

**Q:** What do you get if Bach falls off a horse but has the courage to get on again and continue riding?

**A:** Bach in the saddle again.

**Q:** Why is a violinist like a Scud missile?

**A:** Both are offensive and inaccurate.

**Q:** What do a viola and lawsuits have in common?

**A:** Everyone is happy when the case is closed.

**Q:** How can you tell when a tenor is really stupid?

**A:** When the other tenors notice.

**Q:** What is the most musical bone in the body?

A: The trom-bone.


**Q:** Why don't violists play hide and seek?

A: Because no one will look for them.


**Q:** How do you make a violin sound like a viola?

A: Sit in the back and don't play.


**Q:** What is the best recording of the Walton viola concerto?

A: Music Minus One.

**Q:** What is the difference between a trombone and a trumpet?

**A:** A trombone will bend before it breaks.

**Q:** How can you tell which kid belongs to a trombone player?

**A:** He complains about the slide and he can't swing.

**Q:** How do you make a trombone sound like a French horn?

**A:** Stick your hand in the bell and play lots of wrong notes.

**Q:** How can you tell if a violin is out of tune?

**A:** The bow is moving.

**Q:** What do you get when you drop a piano on an army?

**A:** A flat major.

**Q:** Why are most soprano jokes one-liners?

**A:** So the tenors can understand them.

**Q:** Did you hear about the musician crime wave?

**A:** Drive-by recitals.

**Q:** What is the difference between a violist and a terrorist?

**A:** Terrorists have sympathizers.

**Q:** Why does a viola burn longer than a violin?

A: It is usually still in the case.


**Q:** What is the difference between a trumpet soloist and King Kong?

A: King Kong is more sensitive.


**Q:** Why was the soprano standing outside the door?

A: She forgot the key.


**Q:** What do you call a singing elf?

A: A wrapper.


**Q:** What do you call a person who plays the viola?

A: A violator.

**Q:** How many punk rockers does it take to change a light bulb?

**A:** Two. One to change it and the other to smash the old bulb.

**Q:** What is a bassoon good for?

**A:** Fire wood.

**Q:** What did Mozart's ghost say to visitor of his tomb?

**A:** I'm decomposing!

**Q:** How do lead guitarists change a light bulb?

**A:** They just steal someone else's.

**Q:** What do you call a musician with a college degree?

A: Night Manager at a burger joint.

# ABOUT THE AUTHOR

# LOL
## FUNNY JOKES CLUB

The LOL Funny Jokes Club is dedicated to comedy. We'll tickle your funny bone with our side-splitting jokes and humor. Whether it's funny and hilarious one-liners, hilarious jokes, or laugh-out-loud rib tickling knee slappers, the LOL Funny Jokes Club does it all!

For more funny joke books search for LOL FUNNY JOKES CLUB on Amazon

Printed in Great Britain
by Amazon

# DEDICATION

This book is dedicated everyone in the world that enjoys a good laugh. Laughter is one of the best gifts you can give. It always puts a smile on your face, warms your heart, and makes you feel great.

# Music Jokes

LOL Funny Jokes Club